Animals and Us

FUSION

EXPERT Animals

By E. C. Andrews

BEARPORT PUBLISHING

Minneapolis, Minnesota

Credits
All images are courtesy of Shutterstock.com, unless otherwise specified. With thanks to Getty Images, Thinkstock Photo, and iStockphoto. Recurring – crazyfahh. Cover – lidian Neeleman. TOC – sonsedskaya. 4–5 – Anna Krivitskaya, Monkey Business Images. 6–7 – SeventyFour, Arnbeg Farmstay Scotland. 8–9 – Philippe 1 bo, William Kuhl Photographs, UliAb. 10–11 – Rosa Jay, Adi Haririe, GARY ROBERTS/AlamyStockPhoto. 12–13 – dcurzon, Olga Pysarenko, Yasmins world. 14–15 – TommyStockProject, SeventyFour. 16–17 – PeopleImages, WilleeCole Photography. 18–19 – Dragosh Co, Pixel-Shot, Leeloona. 20–21 – Fertnig, Kachalkina Veronika. 22–23 – Couperfield, Kathrin Ziegler.

Bearport Publishing Company Product Development Team
Publisher: Jen Jenson; Director of Product Development: Spencer Brinker; Managing Editor: Allison Juda; Editor: Cole Nelson; Associate Editor: Naomi Reich; Associate Editor: Tiana Tran; Art Director: Colin O'Dea; Designer: Kim Jones; Designer: Kayla Eggert; Product Development Specialist: Owen Hamlin

Library of Congress Cataloging-in-Publication Data is available at www.loc.gov or upon request from the publisher.

ISBN: 979-8-89232-729-9 (hardcover)
ISBN: 979-8-89232-779-4 (paperback)
ISBN: 979-8-89232-816-6 (ebook)

For more information, write to Bearport Publishing, 5357 Penn Avenue South, Minneapolis, MN 55419.

Contents

WHAT ARE Expert Animals?

There are many kinds of working animals that help us in a lot of ways. But some jobs are harder than others. They need special skills. This is when we need **expert** animals!

Expert animals use their senses or bodies in special ways. Some help solve **crimes**. Others can do tricky jobs or find things that people cannot.

Other types of working animals include guard and service animals.

A Special Kind of Animal

Not all animals can be experts. Along with having strong senses or super smarts, expert animals need to work well with people and be fast learners.

Each special job has to have its own special training.

A lot of training is needed for every expert animal job. A **handler** and an animal act as a team to learn the skills needed. Then, the animal experts are ready to work.

TRUFFLE Pigs

Truffles are a type of **fungus** people use in fancy cooking. They grow underground, so truffles are hard for people to find. However, some pigs can find them deep in the soil.

First, a truffle pig sniffs the area for the fungus. Once truffles are found, the expert animal uses its nose to dig for them. Then, the handler can pick up the truffles.

A handler needs to grab the truffles quickly before the pig eats them.

BOMB Rats

During wars, **explosives** may get buried underground. Some are left there after a war ends. But the bombs can still go off when something heavy presses down on them. That's where rats come in!

Bombs can blow up with a lot of force.

Many rats start training when they are about four or five weeks old.

Rats are too light to set off the explosives. They use their strong noses to sniff out the danger. If they smell something, they scratch at the area to let their handler know there may be a bomb.

CABLE Ferrets

Wires are used to help power buildings.

Sometimes, builders need to run cables with wires through small tunnels. The long, skinny bodies of ferrets can easily get through these places that are hard to reach.

A ferret's handler puts them in a harness with a cable attached. Then, they let the animal follow its natural **instinct** to crawl through the pipe, pulling the cable as it goes.

One cable ferret ran through a tunnel that was 130 feet (40 m) long.

MEDICAL Dogs

Dogs have a great sense of smell. This makes them perfect for medical jobs. Some expert dogs can find an illness just by sniffing a person's breath or sweat.

Medical alert dogs stay with their owners at all times.

Some people have illnesses that can quickly get worse. Medical alert dogs can smell when an **emergency** is about to happen. They let their owners know about the problem.

To become a medical dog, the animal needs a lot of training. It is taught to recognize certain scents by sniffing **samples**.

Trained dogs get lots of hugs whenever they find the correct smell.

Many medical dogs are trained to smell the patient's breath or sweat. This helps dogs notice a change in smell. Then, they learn how to let their handlers know.

Medical dogs may nudge or jump on their handlers when something is wrong.

CRIME Dogs

Crime dogs are expert animals that help the police. They use their strong noses to find things that are against the law. These animal helpers can also look for missing people.

Some crime dogs work in airports. They walk around with their handlers to look for dangerous items. These animal experts sniff people's bags for anything that should not be on an airplane.

When the dogs find something, they sit next to it to let their handlers know.

A crime dog needs to be trained by the handler they will be working with on the job. This makes it easier for the two to **communicate** and work as a team.

Handlers make training fun by rewarding hard work with treats!

Crime dogs practice on different courses.

Sometimes, life on the police force is hard. Crime dogs must learn how to stay calm and patient while working. They are taught to quickly let their handlers know of any danger.

Expert Animals AND US

There are many kinds of expert animals that help us in different ways. They play an important role in keeping us safe, solving problems, and making our lives easier.

Give working animals space to do their jobs.

Always treat working animals with love and respect. Taking good care of these animals helps them stay strong, happy, and healthy while they work.

Glossary

alert to warn someone of danger

communicate to share thoughts, ideas, or information

crimes things that are against the law

emergency a dangerous situation that must be dealt with immediately

expert someone who is highly skilled

explosives things that can blow up

fungus a plantlike living thing that can't make its own food

handler a person who trains and works with animals

instinct knowledge or a way of acting that an animal is born with

samples small bits of things that show what the whole thing will be like

Index